Grandma Alma's Special Room

Patricia Almada

Illustrated by Monique Passicot

Rigby®

A Harcourt Achieve Imprint

www.Rigby.com
1-800-531-5015

This is Grandma Alma's special room.
Carlos and Omar like to watch her work.

Grandma likes to paint pictures.
Sometimes she cuts tissue paper,
or she makes things with paper or clay.

One day Grandma said,

"Omar, please don't come in today."

Omar was very sad.

He wanted to see what Grandma was doing.

Grandma said, "Don't feel sad.

Maybe Grandpa Roberto needs your help."

Omar went outside to help Grandpa Roberto
in the garden.

"Why can't I watch Grandma Alma today?"
asked Omar.

"Maybe tomorrow but not today.
Always listen to your Grandma,"
said Grandpa Roberto.
"Maybe your sister needs your help."

Omar went to Dora's room.
Dora put a big box under her bed.

"Why can't I watch Grandma Alma today?"
asked Omar.

"Maybe tomorrow but not today.

Always listen to Grandma Alma," said Dora.

"Maybe Dad needs your help."

Omar went outside to help Dad with the car.
"Why can't I watch Grandma Alma today?"
asked Omar.

"Maybe tomorrow but not today.
Always listen to your Grandma," said Dad.

That night Omar went to bed a little sad. "Tomorrow will be a better day," said Mom.

In the morning, Omar heard
everyone singing.

Omar jumped out of bed.

"It's my birthday!" he said.

"Now you can see my special room,"
said Grandma Alma.
"I have something for you."

"Carlos helped me make this piñata
just for you," said Grandma Alma.
Omar smiled.

"I will always listen to you, Grandma Alma," he said.